# Nova Latina
## Book 1

# Specimen Answers

R C Bass

Nova Latina Book 1 Specimen Answers

© R C Bass 2021

First published: April 2021

ISBN 979 8 7228054 2 3

All rights reserved. Subject to the exception immediately following, this book may not be reproduced, in whole or in part, in any form, without written permission from the publisher.

The author has made an online version of this work available via email as a free pdf download under a Creative Commons Attribution-NonCommercial-Share Alike 4.0 International Public Licence. The terms of the licence can be viewed at http://creativecommons.org

Also available:
Nova Latina Book 1 ISBN 979 8 5991905 3 0
Streamlined Greek ISBN 978 0 9576725 8 1
Streamlined Greek Answer Book ISBN 978 0 9576725 9 8
Prep School Greek: A workbook leading to CE Level 1 ISBN 978 0 9576725 7 4
More Prep School Greek: A workbook leading to CE Level 2 ISBN 978 1 5272261 3 5
Latin as an Honour Book 1 ISBN 978 0 9576725 0 5
Latin as an Honour Book 2 ISBN 978 0 9576725 3 6
Latin as an Honour Book 3 ISBN 978 0 9576725 4 3
Latin as an Honour Answer Book ISBN 978 0 9576725 5 0
Prep School Latin Book 1 ISBN 978 1 0897232 2 6
Prep School Latin Book 2 ISBN 978 1 6871152 0 1
Prep School Latin Book 3 ISBN 978 1 6871929 2 9
Prep School Latin Book 4 ISBN 978 1 6887813 1 3
Prep School Latin: A Handbook for Students and Teachers ISBN 978 0 9576725 6 7

Published by Galore Park:
Latin Vocabulary for Key Stage 3 ISBN 978 0 9036276 6 5
Latin Pocket Notes ISBN 978 1 9070477 1 8

Typeset by R C Bass

# Introduction

This companion booklet to Nova Latina Book 1 is aimed at autodidacts who do not have access to a specialist teacher, and at teachers who may wish to encourage occasional sensible self-assessment among their pupils.

There is usually more than one way of translating a sentence into or out of Latin, and to provide a comprehensive set of all the possible permutations of Latin word order or English alternatives is simply impracticable; hence the use of 'specimen' in this modest production of suggested answers.

It may be worth drawing attention to the following:

I have adopted the use of the masculine pronoun as the default in the third person singular of verbs, *she* or *it* being, of course, possible alternatives according to context.

The Latin present tense embraces both the English simple present and the present continuous. So, *clamat* may be translated as both 'he shouts' or 'he is shouting.'

Similarly, the imperfect tense can be rendered in a variety of ways in English. So *clamabat* may be translated as 'he was shouting' or 'he used to shout' or 'he would shout.'

The Latin perfect tense encompasses both the English simple past ('preterite' or 'aorist') as well as the 'true' perfect. So *clamavit* may be translated as 'he shouted' or 'he has shouted.'

There is no definite or indefinite article in Latin; *puella* could mean 'a girl' or 'the girl', and *puellae* could mean 'the girls' or simply 'girls' (in general).

Latin does not always specify possessives where an English possessive can be assumed. So, it would be reasonable to translate *femina maritum amat* as 'The woman loves *her* husband.'

R C Bass
robertcharlesbass@gmail.com
rcbass.co.uk

# Contents

|  | page |
|---|---|
| Exercises 2.1 – 3.2 | 1 |
| Exercises 3.3 – 3.11 | 2 |
| Exercises 4.1 – 6.2 | 3 |
| | |
| Exercises 7.1 – 9.3 | 4 |
| Exercises 9.4 – 10.6 | 5 |
| Exercises 11.1 – 13.3 | 6 |
| | |
| Exercises 13.4 – 15.3 | 7 |
| Exercises 15.4 – 15.13 | 8 |
| Exercises 15.14 – 17.1 | 9 |
| | |
| Exercises 17.2 – 19.1 | 10 |
| Exercises 19.2 – 21.6 | 11 |
| Exercises 22.1 – 23.4 | 12 |
| | |
| Exercises 24.1 – 25.2 | 13 |
| Exercises 26.1 – 27.2 | 14 |
| Exercises 28.1 – 28.8 | 15 |
| | |
| Exercises 28.9 – 29.2 | 16 |
| Exercises 30.1 – 32.3 | 17 |
| Exercises 32.4 – 33.2 | 18 |
| | |
| Exercises 34.1 – 35.2 | 19 |
| Exercises 36.1 – 37.2 | 20 |
| Exercises 38.1 – 38.2; Tests 1 – 8 | 21 |
| Tests 9 – 18 | 22 |

# Nova Latina 1 Specimen Answers

## Exercise 2.1
1. amat.
2. ambulant.
3. cantas.
4. clamat.
5. habitat.
6. spectatis.
7. spectamus.
8. clamant.
9. ambulamus.
10. amant.

## Exercise 2.2
1. spectamus.
2. cantat.
3. specto.
4. cantant.
5. clamamus.
6. habitant.
7. ambulat.
8. spectant.
9. amat.
10. spectant.

## Exercise 2.3
1. amamus.
2. ambulo.
3. cantas.
4. ambulas.
5. habitatis.
6. cantamus.
7. spectat.
8. clamo.
9. amatis.
10. habitamus.

Reminder: If the Latin verb ends in -at, *she* and *it* are possible alternatives to *he* !

## Exercise 2.4
1. spectat.
2. amo.
3. habitas.
4. ambulamus.
5. cantatis.
6. clamant.
7. canto.
8. spectant.
9. habitat.
10. ambulant.

## Exercise 2.5
1. clamat.
2. habitant.
3. spectamus.
4. amas.
5. specto.
6. clamatis.
7. amant.
8. clamas.
9. habito.
10. ambulatis.

## Exercise 2.6
1. You live.
2. You sing.
3. I like.
4. He is watching.
5. You are walking.
6. They shout.
7. He lives.
8. You like.
9. He shouts.
10. They watch.

## Exercise 2.7
1. You are walking.
2. They like.
3. You shout.
4. I am singing.
5. They live.
6. We walk.
7. You watch.
8. I am walking.
9. We like.
10. He is singing.

## Exercise 2.8
1. You are watching.
2. They are walking.
3. He lives.
4. I shout.
5. You are watching.
6. We sing.
7. He walks.
8. You live.
9. We are watching.
10. You shout.

## Exercise 3.1
1. puella spectat.
2. regina amat.
3. nauta clamat.
4. filia cantat.
5. agricola habitat.

## Exercise 3.2
1. femina ambulat.
2. domina clamat.
3. nauta cantat.
4. regina spectat.
5. filia ambulat.

3.3 – 3.11  Nova Latina 1 Specimen Answers

### Exercise 3.3
1. agricola clamat.
2. puella cantat.
3. domina spectat.
4. agricola ambulat.
5. nauta ambulat.
6. filia amat.
7. femina clamat.
8. puella ambulat.
9. regina clamat.
10. agricola cantat.

### Exercise 3.4
1. The mistress is shouting.
2. The queen lives.
3. The girl is singing.
4. The mistress is singing.
5. The daughter is watching.
6. The farmer likes.
7. The sailor is walking.
8. The woman is shouting.
9. The girl is watching.
10. The queen is walking.

### Exercise 3.5
1. The inhabitant is shouting.
2. The inhabitants are shouting.
3. The goddess is singing.
4. The goddesses are singing.
5. The maidservants are working.
6. The maidservant is working.
7. The sailors are fighting.
8. The sailor is fighting.
9. The maidservant is sailing.
10. The maidservants are sailing.

### Exercise 3.6
1. The goddess is shouting.
2. The goddesses are shouting.
3. The sailors are sailing.
4. The sailor is sailing.
5. The mistress is shouting.
6. The goddesses are watching.
7. The girls hurry.
8. The farmer enters.
9. The daughters are singing.
10. The queen is walking.

### Exercise 3.7
1. dea cantat.
2. deae cantant.
3. regina intrat.
4. reginae intrant.
5. nautae pugnant.
6. ancilla spectat.
7. agricolae festinant.
8. incolae laborant.
9. nauta navigat.
10. dominae clamant.

### Exercise 3.8
1. filia clamat.
2. nautae pugnant.
3. incolae cantant.
4. puella pugnat.
5. ancilla laborat.
6. feminae festinant.
7. puella intrat.
8. agricolae spectant.
9. regina ambulat.
10. dominae navigant.

### Exercise 3.9
1. domina clamat.
2. puellae spectant.
3. agricola laborat.
4. dea cantat.
5. filiae festinant.
6. reginae clamant.
7. nautae navigant.
8. femina laborat.
9. deae pugnant.
10. incola intrat,

### Exercise 3.10
1. deae clamant.
2. agricolae pugnant.
3. filia cantat.
4. incolae pugnant.
5. ancillae laborant.
6. puellae navigant.
7. domina cantat.
8. feminae pugnant.
9. femina clamat.
10. incola laborat.

### Exercise 3.11
1. nautae ambulant.
2. agricola clamat.
3. dea spectat.
4. puellae laborant.
5. deae festinant.
6. puella festinat.
7. femina intrat.
8. nauta pugnat.
9. domina spectat.
10. agricolae cantant.

# Nova Latina 1 Specimen Answers  4.1 – 6.2

## Exercise 4.1
1. cantant. They sing.
2. habitat. He lives.
3. habitas. You live.
4. festinas. You hurry.
5. ambulamus. We walk.
6. portant. They carry.
7. navigas. You sail.
8. intratis. You enter.
9. clamat. He shouts.
10. amant. They like.
11. cantamus. We sing.

## Exercise 4.2
1. You work. 2nd person plural.
2. You sing. 2nd person singular.
3. They shout. 3rd person plural.
4. We fight. 1st person singular.
5. He enters. 3rd person singular.
6. He lives. 3rd person singular.
7. They like. 3rd person plural.
8. You hurry. 2nd person plural.
9. You carry. 2nd person singular.
10. He walks. 3rd person singular.
11. We watch. 1st person plural.

## Exercise 5.1
1. villam aedificamus.
2. reginam laudant.
3. cenam parat.
4. pecuniam amo.
5. silvam intratis.
6. aquam spectat.
7. dominam necamus.
8. hastam paras.
9. ancillam vocat.
10. deam laudo.

## Exercise 5.2
1. villam specto.
2. reginam amamus.
3. villam intrant.
4. nautam vocamus.
5. feminam necat.
6. ancillam vocas.
7. cenam parat.
8. agricolam laudant.
9. villam aedificatis.
10. hastam amat.

## Exercise 5.3
1. He likes money.
2. I enter the water.
3. You praise the goddess.
4. We like the dinner.
5. He enters the villa.
6. You call the mistress.
7. They kill the queen.
8. You enter the wood.
9. They call the maidservant.
10. We look at the sailor.

## Exercise 5.4
1. puella cantat.
2. puellam amamus.
3. domina vocat.
4. dominam laudamus.
5. ancilla clamat.
6. ancillam vocas.
7. pecuniam spectant.
8. cenam paramus.
9. filia laborat.
10. villam intratis.

## Exercise 5.5
1. The mistress is calling.
2. The mistresses are calling.
3. We like the mistress.
4. Sailors sail.
5. You praise the sailor.
6. The queen is singing.
7. The maidservants are working.
8. They are calling the maidservant.
9. You are preparing dinner.
10. The women are shouting.

## Exercise 6.1
1. nautae insulam oppugnant.
2. femina sagittam portat.
3. incolae patriam amant.
4. puellae pecuniam rogant.
5. agricolae viam aedificant.
6. domina ancillam superat.
7. turba puellam spectat.
8. poeta aquam rogat.
9. sagittae feminam superant.
10. poetae sagittam spectant.

## Exercise 6.2
1. The farmer is carrying his daughter.
2. The inhabitants are asking for dinner.
3. The poet praises the country.
4. The sailors like money.
5. The women are watching the sailor.
6. The crowd kills the poet.
7. The inhabitants praise the queen.
8. Sailors like water.
9. The crowd praises the country.
10. The poet is preparing dinner.

## Exercise 7.1

1. You are calling the maidservants.
2. We praise the poet.
3. The inhabitants are shouting.
4. You enter the woods.
5. He is asking for water.
6. He is building roads.
7. The poet is working.
8. We are watching the crowd.
9. They are preparing spears.
10. I am looking at the maidservant.

## Exercise 7.2

1. puella poetam amat.
2. puella poetas amat.
3. puellae poetam amant.
4. puellae poetas amant.
5. dominae ancillam spectant.
6. domina ancillas spectat.
7. domina ancillas spectat. (!)
8. dominae ancillas spectant.
9. regina incolas laudat.
10. nautae sagittas parant.

## Exercise 7.3

1. The farmer loves the maidservant.
2. The farmer loves the maidservants.
3. The farmers love the maidservant.
4. The farmers love the maidservants.
5. The daughter enters the wood.
6. The inhabitants are building roads.
7. The poet praises the goddesses.
8. The sailors are carrying spears.
9. The mistress is calling the maidservants.
10. The maidservants are watching the mistress.

## Exercise 8.1

1. saepe festinas.
2. semper bene laboramus.
3. agricolae saepe pugnant.
4. numquam diu laborat.
5. puellae semper bene cantant.
6. agricola semper bene laborat.
7. ancillae saepe festinant.
8. nautae bene cantant.
9. nautae numquam bene cantant.
10. poeta non semper bene laborat.

## Exercise 9.1

1. We warn.
2. He has.
3. You frighten.
4. They hold.
5. He sees.
6. You destroy.
7. They move.
8. I frighten.
9. We fear.
10. We hold.

## Exercise 9.2

1. He holds.
2. You see.
3. I fear.
4. They have.
5. You see.
6. You warn.
7. He warns.
8. You frighten.
9. We move.
10. They destroy.

## Exercise 9.3

1. The sailors do not fear.
2. You move the money.
3. Arrows destroy.
4. The girl fears.
5. I am warning the sailor.
6. We move the spears.
7. We frighten the girls.
8. I have a daughter.
9. They are holding spears.
10. You see the villa.

## Exercise 9.4

1. The girls fear/are afraid.
2. The maidservant fears the mistress.
3. The queen warns the inhabitants.
4. The crowd frightens the girl.
5. The sailors destroy the island.
6. The farmer is holding a spear.
7. The women fear the sailors.
8. The water does not frighten the sailor.
9. The mistress has a daughter.
10. The poet destroys the letter.

## Exercise 9.5

1. timent.
2. habemus.
3. vides.
4. tenet.
5. delemus.
6. monent.
7. terretis.
8. timeo.
9. movemus.
10. videt.

## Exercise 9.6

1. puella timet.
2. insulam video.
3. hastas tenemus.
4. pecuniam movet.
5. filias habent.
6. nautas times.
7. epistulam videmus.
8. aquam tenet.
9. incolas monet.
10. reginam videtis.

## Exercise 10.1

1. amamus. We like.
2. mones. You warn.
3. laborat. He works.
4. timent. They fear.
5. festinatis. You hurry.
6. oppugnas. You attack.
7. deleo. I destroy.
8. habitamus. We live.
9. cantant. They sing.
10. videt. He sees.

## Exercise 10.2

1. deletis.
2. tenemus.
3. navigant.
4. times.
5. specto.
6. laudat.
7. habet.
8. videmus.
9. superamus.
10. pugnant.

## Exercise 10.3

1. sagittae delent.
2. poeta timet.
3. dominae monent.
4. agricolae bene pugnant.
5. ancillae vident.
6. reginae non timent.
7. nauta numquam cantat.
8. turba laborat.
9. nautae saepe navigant.
10. puella et femina festinant.

## Exercise 10.4

1. pecuniam habent.
2. deam laudamus.
3. cenam parat.
4. ancillas terretis.
5. puellas amat.
6. reginam rogamus.
7. incolas moneo.
8. villam aedificas.
9. epistulam spectant.
10. silvam intramus.

## Exercise 10.5

1. A queen always has money.
2. Sailors never work well.
3. The farmer often carries spears and arrows.
4. Girls never build roads well.
5. The mistress does not often frighten the maidservants.

## Exercise 10.6

1. puellae sagittas semper timent.
2. ancillae pecuniam numquam habent.
3. poetae feminas saepe timent.
4. nautae hastas numquam bene parant.
5. regina puellas saepe terret.

## Exercise 11.1

1. You are sailors.
2. He is a farmer.
3. She is not a goddess.
4. They are women.
5. She is the queen.
6. You are a sailor.
7. I am the queen.
8. We are inhabitants.
9. It is a letter.
10. They are arrows.

## Exercise 11.2

1. ancilla est.
2. agricolae sumus.
3. poeta es.
4. nautae estis.
5. feminae sumus.
6. villa est.
7. hastae sunt.
8. ancilla non es.
9. nauta est.
10. agricolae non sumus.

## Exercise 11.3

1. nauta poeta est.
2. femina regina est.
3. regina ancilla non est.
4. ancilla regina non saepe est.
5. incolae agricolae saepe sunt.

## Exercise 12.1

1. pecunia reginae.
2. pecunia reginarum.
3. filiae nautae.
4. filiae nautarum.
5. incolae insulae.
6. turba ancillarum.
7. hasta agricolae.
8. regina insulae.
9. sagittae agricolarum.
10. ancilla poetae.

## Exercise 12.2

1. incolae insulae semper bene pugnant.
2. dea insulae incolas numquam terret.
3. filia agricolae ancilla est.
4. nautae villam reginae numquam oppugnant.
5. ancillae poetae pecuniam nautarum amant.

## Exercise 12.4

Britain is an island. Britain is a big island. Many inhabitants live in Britain. They love their own country. They work well. They build roads and villas. Because they love Britain, they are happy.

Julius Caesar is a Roman. He does not like the inhabitants of Britain. Therefore he calls sailors. The sailors prepare arrows and spears, sail across the water and attack Britain. When the crowds of inhabitants see the Romans, they are afraid.

## Exercise 13.1

1. hearts: genitive. tarts: accusative.
2. teacher: nominative. Mars Bar: ablative.
3. We: nominative. taxi: ablative.
4. Girl: vocative. room: ablative.
5. you: nominative. me: dative.

## Exercise 13.2

1. teacher: nominative. boy: accusative.
2. Boy: vocative. you: nominative.
3. boy: accusative. stick: ablative.
4. sir: vocative. boy: nominative.
5. master: nominative. boy: dative.

## Exercise 13.3

1. teachers: dative.
2. Work: nominative.
3. mist: ablative.
4. Boy: vocative. cigarette: accusative.
5. help: ablative. public: genitive. police: nominative. dog: accusative. owner: dative.

# Nova Latina 1 Specimen Answers    13.4 – 15.3

### Exercise 13.4
1. epistulis
2. ira
3. villae
4. aqua
5. pecuniae
6. terra
7. incolis
8. nautis
9. puellae
10. cenae

### Exercise 13.5
1. filiae
2. via
3. insulis
4. sagittis
5. dominae
6. feminis
7. ancillis
8. epistula
9. reginae
10. reginis

### Exercise 13.6
1. dominae ancillarum
2. reginae Graeciae
3. sagittis incolarum
4. ira deae
5. epistula poetae
6. filiae feminae
7. cenae agricolae
8. pecunia reginae
9. incolis patriae
10. turbis puellarum

### Exercise 14.1
1. Maidservant, why do you not always work well?
2. The mistress gives money to the maidservant.
3. Why do you fear sailors, girls?
4. We fear sailors because we do not like sailors.
5. The crowd of sailors is attacking the inhabitants of the island with spears.

### Exercise 14.2
1. The sailors attack Troy immediately.
2. The woman asks her daughter, but her daughter does not reply.
3. The farmers are frightening the girls with spears.
4. The sailor is building a road for the inhabitants.
5. The sailors give spears to the inhabitants of the land.

### Exercise 14.3
1. femina cenam filiae parat.
2. aquam incolis saepe do.
3. cenam puellis paramus.
4. poeta epistulam reginae statim dat.
5. villas hastis deletis, agricolae.

### Exercise 14.4
1. ancillae reginae non bene respondet.
2. nautae, cur Romam hastis oppugnatis?
3. domina pecuniam ancillis numquam dat.
4. incolae Graeciae semper bene pugnant.
5. insulam hastis nautarum oppugnamus.

### Exercise 15.1
1. regit.
2. mittitis.
3. discedunt.
4. venio.
5. dormimus.
6. curris.
7. legunt.
8. scribit.
9. bibimus.
10. auditis.

### Exercise 15.2
1. You read.
2. We send.
3. He sleeps.
4. They come.
5. You write.
6. I depart.
7. They drink.
8. He sends.
9. They write.
10. I hear.

### Exercise 15.3
1. The sailor is drinking.
2. The inhabitants are running.
3. The girl is reading.
4. The poets are writing.
5. The farmers are departing.
6. We hear the queen.
7. You are writing a letter.
8. I am drinking water.
9. They are sending money.
10. The girls are sleeping.

# Nova Latina 1 Specimen Answers

## Exercise 15.4

1. regina regit.
2. agricolae veniunt.
3. incolae dormiunt.
4. nautae bibunt.
5. epistulam legis.
6. aquam bibit.
7. epistulas scribunt.
8. deam audimus.
9. pecuniam mittit.
10. terram regunt.

## Exercise 15.5

1. Poets do not always write letters well.
2. The crowd of sailors is departing immediately.
3. Sailors do not often drink water.
4. Why are you reading a letter, girl?
5. The queen always rules Troy well.

## Exercise 15.6

1. nautae saepe pugnant.
2. cur curritis, puellae?
3. currimus quod deam timemus.
4. ancillae dominam semper audiunt.
5. agricolae statim discedunt.
6. poeta Romam magnopere amat.
7. incolae non semper bene currunt.
8. cur semper dormis, ancilla?
9. poetae epistulas semper scribunt.
10. feminae numquam diu bibunt.

## Exercise 15.7

1. They like.
2. You destroy.
3. He runs.
4. He comes.
5. They are.
6. You give.
7. You rule.
8. He sees.
9. You work.
10. You kill.

## Exercise 15.8

1. They run.
2. You praise.
3. We are.
4. You hear.
5. You watch.
6. He replies.
7. I hold.
8. He writes.
9. You carry.
10. They fear.

## Exercise 15.9

1. He fears.
2. He enters.
3. You are.
4. We send.
5. I call.
6. He reads.
7. They write.
8. They attack.
9. We warn.
10. You drink.

## Exercise 15.10

1. We see.
2. I shout.
3. They reply.
4. You are.
5. You sleep.
6. He lives.
7. He has.
8. They overcome.
9. They come.
10. You frighten.

## Exercise 15.11

1. We build.
2. You move.
3. You depart.
4. You hurry.
5. He is.
6. He fights.
7. I am.
8. We ask.
9. You walk.
10. They hold.

## Exercise 15.12

1. timet.
2. respondent.
3. dat.
4. laudant.
5. regimus.
6. dormis.
7. scribimus.
8. oppugnat.
9. sumus.
10. discedunt.

## Exercise 15.13

1. sunt.
2. videt.
3. clamas.
4. vocant.
5. respondemus.
6. mittit.
7. scribo.
8. venimus.
9. dormitis.
10. audiunt.

## Exercise 15.14

1. necamus.
2. rogat.
3. pugnamus.
4. navigant.
5. laudat.
6. intras.
7. festino.
8. laboratis.
9. vident.
10. est.

## Exercise 15.15

1. es.
2. audimus.
3. curro.
4. bibit.
5. regitis.
6. respondet.
7. times.
8. parat.
9. laudamus.
10. rogant.

## Exercise 15.16

1. estis.
2. dormit.
3. scribimus.
4. veniunt.
5. video.
6. terres.
7. ambulamus.
8. habitamus.
9. scribunt.
10. laborat.

## Exercise 16.1

1. servi
2. cibo
3. amici!
4. deo
5. dominis
6. equi
7. filio
8. muris
9. gladio
10. marito

## Exercise 16.2

1. The horse is running.
2. We fear the gods
3. I have a husband.
4. They are preparing swords.
5. The friends are shouting.
6. He does not have food.
7. The slaves are sleeping.
8. We are building a wall.
9. The son is not listening.
10. Friends are coming.

## Exercise 16.3

1. The queen does not have a husband.
2. The slaves are attacking the walls.
3. Maidservants do not have friends.
4. Why do we always fear the gods?
5. The farmer likes food.
6. Girls love horses.
7. Slaves often fear their masters.
8. The son is holding a sword and a spear.
9. Husband, why do you not love your son?
10. We are attacking the wall with swords.

## Exercise 16.4

1. Slaves do not always like their masters.
2. Slaves, why do you fear the gods?
3. Farmers often carry spears.
4. We are looking at the queen's horses.
5. Queens do not always have husbands.
6. Girls often give food to horses.
7. Friend, why are you giving food to the slave?
8. A crowd of slaves is coming.
9. The husband of the queen always carries a sword.
10. Women often ask their husbands for money.

## Exercise 16.5

1. ancillae dominum timent.
2. domini servos numquam audiunt.
3. servus cibum equo parat.
4. equus domini aquam semper bibit.
5. servi villam gladiis oppugnant.

## Exercise 17.1

The Britons are standing on the shore. They are looking at the Romans. The Britons do not like the Romans and the Romans do not like the Britons. When the Romans prepare their swords and spears and horses they run towards the Britons. They shout. The Romans and the Britons fight bravely and for a long time. The Romans kill many Britons with their swords and spears. Finally the Britons, because they are tired, flee. The Romans are now happy. They laugh. Caesar praises the Romans because they fight well.

## Exercise 17.2

1. a. stant/spectant/amant/parant/clamant/pugnant/necat/laudat
   b. rident
   c. currunt
   d. non/fortiter/diu/iam/bene
2. stant means 'stand' and stationary describes something that is standing still.
3. 3rd person. Plural.
4. Accusative
5. Romani

## Exercise 17.3

1. When the sailors attack, they shout.
2. When the poet sees the queen, he is afraid.
3. Because the sailors are attacking, the inhabitants are afraid.
4. When the slaves destroy the villa they depart.
5. Because they love their country the inhabitants do not depart.
6. When the master calls, the slave always comes immediately.
7. Because she fears the anger of the queen, the woman departs.
8. When the maidservants are preparing dinner they never sing.
9. When the master frightens the slaves he laughs.
10. When the women see the crowd of sailors they are afraid.

## Exercise 18.1

1. down from the wall
2. out of the villa
3. with friends
4. near the road
5. in the letter
6. against the slaves
7. away from the island
8. across the road
9. into the villa
10. towards the crowd

## Exercise 18.2

1. in muro
2. in villa
3. in villam
4. cum amicis
5. in epistula
6. prope insulas
7. contra equos
8. per viam
9. per silvas
10. ex villis

## Exercise 18.3

1. I am drinking in the villa.
2. We are sailing away from the island.
3. Why are you running across the road, girl?
4. The woman is hurrying towards her husband.
5. We are fighting against the sailors.
6. The sailors are sleeping on the island.
7. Why are you not departing from the island, sailors?
8. Queens do not often write letters to their friends.
9. The sailor is moving the money out of the villa.
10. Farmers often fight against sailors.

## Exercise 18.4

1. nautae ad insulam navigant.
2. poeta epistulam in villa scribit.
3. agricola murum cum amicis aedificat.
4. domina, cur in villam curris?
5. regina filium ab insula mittit.
6. nautae ab undis numquam currunt.
7. incolae murum in insula aedificant.
8. filia reginae trans viam saepe currit.
9. ancilla cenam in villa domini parat.
10. servi e silvis ad villam currunt.

## Exercise 19.1

1. The man is running.
2. The men are writing.
3. You are a boy.
4. You are reading a book.
5. I do not like the teacher.
6. Teachers often read.
7. The boy is singing.
8. I never write in books.
9. Teachers never frighten boys and girls.
10. Masters never give food to their slaves.

## Exercise 19.2
1. dominus librum legit.
2. pueri magistrum amant.
3. puellae pueros semper amant.
4. vir agrum habet.
5. magister virum terret.

## Exercise 19.3
1. vir magistrum monet.
2. agricolae in agris saepe laborant.
3. librum puero damus.
4. viri in agro stant.
5. turba servorum pueros gladiis terret.

## Exercise 20.1

Rhea is a beautiful woman. She lives in Italy. She has two sons. The sons are small. The father of the sons is the god Mars. But Rhea is not happy. She is not happy because the king of the country, Amulius, does not like the small boys. Because Amulius does not like the small sons of Rhea, he decides to kill them. The names of the boys are Romulus and Remus.

## Exercise 20.2

1. 
   a. habet
   b. est/sunt
   c. in
   d. non
   e. filiorum/patriae/puerorum
2. Ablative. After the preposition *in*.
3. 3rd person. Singular.
4. Genitive.

## Exercise 21.1
1. to live
2. to see
3. to drink
4. to come
5. to send
6. to write
7. to hold
8. to enter
9. to sleep
10. to work

## Exercise 21.2
1. spectare
2. respondere
3. currere
4. legere
5. timere
6. clamare
7. aedificare
8. movere
9. ducere
10. festinare

## Exercise 21.3
1. We are preparing to sing.
2. I want to shout.
3. We like to write.
4. They want to sleep.
5. You decide to drink.

## Exercise 21.4
1. pueros scribere iubent.
2. poeta esse cupio.
3. pueri laborare numquam cupiunt.
4. poeta librum scribere constituit.
5. servi villam oppugnare parant.

## Exercise 21.5
1. I like to read.
2. They are preparing to fight.
3. They decide to fight.
4. He does not want to come.
5. He is preparing to reply.

## Exercise 21.6
1. ad insulam navigare constituimus.
2. viros villam aedificare iubemus.
3. puellae nautae esse numquam cupiunt.
4. domina ancillas laborare iubet.
5. servus equum ex agro currere iubet.

## Exercise 22.1

When Amulius sees Romulus and Remus he is angry. He decides to kill the little boys immediately. Amulius therefore calls his slaves. He orders the slaves to take the boys. He orders the slaves to carry the boys to the river. He orders the slaves to throw the boys into the water. However, because the slaves love the boys, they do not want to do this. But they fear Amulius. They fear Amulius greatly. Therefore they take the boys, they carry them to the river, they throw them into the water. Then they depart.

## Exercise 22.2

1. a. necare/capere/portare/iacere/facere
   b. ad/in
   c. et/sed/tamen
2. Amulius
3. servos
4. Accusative. After the preposition *ad*.
5. 3rd person. Plural.
6. *portant* means 'carry', and portable describes something which can be carried.

## Exercise 23.1

1. Slaves have shields.
2. We are standing in the forum.
3. Farmers always fear wars.
4. Slave, why are you carrying gold?
5. We never drink the master's wine.
6. Men often kill slaves in war.
7. The sailors are attacking the walls of the town.
8. With the help of the slaves we are building a villa.
9. The poet is writing a book in the temple.
10. We never listen to the teacher's words.

## Exercise 23.2

1. pericula belli timemus.
2. puellae scuta non portant.
3. agricolae, cur caelum spectatis?
4. viri vinum pueris non dant.
5. vir ex templo in forum festinat.

## Exercise 23.3

1. The inhabitans are carrying gold out of the temple.
2. We often drink wine in the villa.
3. Inhabitants, why are you asking for help?
4. Teachers often frighten boys and girls with words.
5. The master is sending help to the slaves.
6. Mistresses do not often give gold to maidservants.
7. The words of teachers often frighten girls.
8. The master likes to have gold.
9. The master throws the maidservant down from the wall.
10. Girl, why are you sleeping in the temple?

## Exercise 23.4

1. vinum amo.
2. oppida in insula sunt.
3. servi ex proelio currunt.
4. templa oppidi spectamus.
5. cur viri in foro pugnant?

## Exercise 24.1

1. Sailors do not fear winds.
2. We are looking at the gardens of the island.
3. The freedman of the master likes money.
4. I never give money to a freedman.
5. The maidservants are hurrying out of the villa into the garden.
6. Masters do not often give gold to freedmen.
7. With the help of the allies we are attacking Troy.
8. Why are you giving money to the prisoners, master?
9. The prisoners are forming a plan in the temple.
10. The allies are killing the inhabitans of Rome with spears and swords.

## Exercise 24.2

1. hortos amamus.
2. servi ex loco currunt.
3. captivus puellas terret.
4. captivi libros non legunt.
5. regina auxilium sociis saepe dat.
6. puella epistulam in horto scribit.
7. puellae epistulas in hortis scribunt.
8. cur captivum laudas, serve?
9. socii auxilium incolis dant.
10. captivos in bello saepe capimus.

## Exercise 24.3

1. nuntius ad oppidum currit.
2. servi in horto laborant.
3. venti et undae nautas non terrent.
4. libertus cum domino in Graecia habitat.
5. socii cum incolis terrae numquam pugnant.

## Exercise 25.1

Romulus and Remus are now in the river. They are very afraid of the water. The water carries the boys along the river. They are in great danger. However, when the gods see the little boys in the river, they decide to save them. The waves soon carry the boys to land and put them there. Because the boys are tired, they sleep on the land. They stay there for a long time. And so Romulus and Remus are now safe.

## Exercise 25.2

1. a. aquam/aqua/undae/terram/terra
   b. timent/vident/manent
   c. et/ubi/quod/itaque
   d. iam/magnopere/tamen/mox/ibi/diu
2. *aqua* means 'water' and an aquarium is a water tank.
3. sum
4. Accusative. Singular.
5. pueri

## Exercise 26.1

1. parva puella
2. parvae puellae
3. vir clarus
4. viri clari
5. verbum malum
6. verba mala
7. dominus/magister iratus
8. domini/magistri/irati
9. magnum templum
10. magna templa

## Exercise 26.2

1. vina bona
2. insula tuta
3. insulae tutae
4. nauta laetus
5. nautae laeti
6. ancilla irata
7. ancillae iratae
8. multi pueri
9. multa scuta
10. multae sagittae

## Exercise 26.3

1. Many boys never work.
2. I often drink good wines.
3. Teachers are often bad.
4. I fear big crowds.
5. We praise the famous poet.
6. The little boys are now safe.
7. We are reading a good book.
8. They are throwing many spears.
9. The farmer has many fields.
10. Sailors fear big waves.

## Exercise 26.4

1. maritum bonum habeo.
2. magnum templum aedificatis.
3. reginam claram laudant.
4. socios bonos habemus.
5. ancillas bonas laudat.

## Exercise 26.5

1. Tired slaves always sleep well.
2. The walls of the town are big.
3. Big winds frighten many sailors.
4. The boys hear the words of the angry master.
5. The boys hear the angry words of the master.
6. I do not have many good friends.
7. We are tired because we are building a big wall.
8. The allies capture many prisoners in the battle.
9. Masters often give money to good slaves.
10. A crowd of angry inhabitants is hurrying towards the forum.

## Exercise 26.6

1. magister pueros malos monet.
2. regina bona filium laetum et filiam laetam habet.
3. servi fessi sunt quod semper laborant.
4. multi viri contra servos in viis pugnant.
5. ancillae cenam bonam viro claro parant.

## Exercise 27.1

Romulus and Remus are on land. The boys drink water, but they do not have food. Therefore they are still in great danger. Near the river lives a she-wolf. When the she-wolf is walking near the river she suddenly sees the two little boys. She decides to save them. She carries Romulus and Remus home. The she-wolf has a good friend. The she-wolf's friend is a woodpecker. The she-wolf and the woodpecker look after the boys for a long time. The she-wolf gives milk, and the woodpecker food, to Romulus and Remus. The boys are now safe and happy.

## Exercise 27.2

1. 
   a. habitat/ambulat/portat/curant/dat
   b. habent/vident/habet
   c. bibunt/constituit
   d. non/igitur/adhuc/subito/diu/iam
2. aquam
3. *habitat* means 'lives' and uninhabitable describes a place where you can't live.
4. Masculine.
5. Dative

# Nova Latina 1 Specimen Answers — 28.1 – 28.8

## Exercise 28.1
1. habitabat.
2. tenebam.
3. bibebant.
4. dormiebas.
5. eramus.
6. habitabant.
7. movebat.
8. legebamus.
9. veniebatis.
10. erat.

## Exercise 28.2
1. pugnabant.
2. spectabam.
3. ponebamus.
4. discedebat.
5. terrebatis.
6. bibebant.
7. currebamus.
8. audiebat.
9. ducebas.
10. iubebant.

## Exercise 28.3
1. He was putting.
2. They were staying.
3. They were departing.
4. He was deciding.
5. I was.
6. They were standing.
7. I was drinking.
8. You were shouting.
9. We were departing.
10. I was sending.

## Exercise 28.4
1. We were drinking.
2. You were writing.
3. They were moving.
4. He was standing.
5. We were.
6. They were sailing.
7. You were holding.
8. He was building.
9. I was seeing.
10. He was ordering.

## Exercise 28.5
1. Troiani fortiter pugnabant.
2. incola per viam ambulabat.
3. agricolae scuta portabant.
4. ancilla pecuniam habebat.
5. puer aquam saepe bibebat.

## Exercise 28.6
1. viri insulam oppugnabant.
2. servi sagittas iaciebant.
3. agricolae deos non timebant.
4. feminae bella non amabant.
5. puellae agricolam amabant.

## Exercise 28.7
1. multi nautae in templo Graeco dormiebant.
2. servi parvos equos in agrum ducebant.
3. puer malus multas puellas magno gladio terrebat.

## Exercise 28.8
1. The mistress had a son and a daughter.
2. We were tired because we were building a wall.
3. The maidservant was preparing a good dinner.
4. You were running along the road.
5. A big crowd was frightening the girls.
6. We were sailing to the island.
7. Many freedmen were staying in the villa.
8. Help was coming.
9. I was drinking water and wine.
10. We were attacking the walls with swords.

## Exercise 28.9

1. The mistress often used to write letters in the garden.
2. The Roman boys were hurrying along the road.
3. We were listening to the teacher.
4. The farmer used to live in the fields.
5. The queen liked money and gold.
6. The slaves were sleeping in the temple.
7. The Trojans were throwing spears and arrows.
8. The sailors would often drink wine in the forum.
9. You were building a villa.
10. The woman often used to ask her husband for money.

## Exercise 28.10

1. The teacher often used to warn the bad boys.
2. The sailors were fighting against the inhabitants in the streets.
3. The mistress was calling the maidservants into the villa.
4. The words of the teacher were frightening the little girls.
5. The horses were running out of the town into the fields.

## Exercise 29.1

Romulus and Remus stayed with the she-wolf and the woodpecker for a long time. One day a shepherd, Faustulus, caught sight of the little boys in the fields. When he saw them he was amazed. He ran to his villa. Here Faustulus used to live with his wife, Acca. He shouted to Acca: 'Acca, come immediately! Run!' Acca replied to Faustulus: 'What is it, Faustulus? Why are you shouting? Answer!' Faustulus replied to Acca: 'I have found two little boys. They are in danger.' Acca replied to Faustulus: 'Where are they, Faustulus?' Faustulus shouted again: 'They are in the fields. Come! Hurry!' And so Faustulus and Acca immediately hurried to the fields. There they found Romulus and Remus and led them to their villa.

## Exercise 29.2

1. a. habitabat/clamavit/clamas/festina!/festinaverunt
   b. in/ad
   c. erat/est/sunt
   d. diu/olim/hic/statim/iterum/ibi
2. *agris* means 'fields' and agriculture refers to farming in the fields.
3. 3rd person. Singular.
4. Dative.
5. Faustulus.

## Exercise 30.1

1. rege, regina!
2. regite, reginae!
3. curre, puer!
4. currite, pueri!
5. oppugna, amice!
6. oppugnate, amici!
7. pugna, serve!
8. pugnate, servi!
9. dormi, puella!
10. dormite, puellae!

## Exercise 30.2

1. vinum bibe, puer!
2. vinum bibite, pueri!
3. murum aedifica, serve!
4. murum aedificate, servi!
5. hastam para, agricola!

## Exercise 30.3

1. Throw spears, farmers!
2. Prepare your shields, slaves!
3. Boy, read a good book!
4. Always fight well, Romans!
5. Kill the inhabitants, sailors!
6. Take the money, boys!
7. Punish the bad maidservant, mistress!
8. Attack the town, sailors!
9. Build a big wall, slave!
10. Listen to the teacher's words, boys!

## Exercise 30.4

1. trans viam curre, puer!
2. bene pugnate in proelio, viri!
3. ab insula navigate, nautae!
4. librum in horto scribe, poeta!
5. villam hastis oppugnate, servi!

## Exercise 31.1

Romulus and Remus were now safe. They lived for a long time in the villa of Acca and Faustulus. Soon the small boys were young men. Finally, because they wanted to build their own new town, they decided to depart from the villa. They therefore approached Acca and Faustulus and said these words: 'Acca and Faustulus, we love you greatly. But we want to depart and build a new town. Our town will be big and beautiful and well known.

## Exercise 31.2

1. 
   a. iam/diu/mox/tandem/igitur/magnopere
   b. aedificare/discedere
   c. in/a
   d. oppidum/verba
2. Imperfect. sum.
3. Genitive.
4. verba
5. Vocative
6. 1st

## Exercise 32.1

1. servus miser
2. servi miseri
3. puella pulchra
4. puellae pulchrae
5. agricola miser
6. agricolae miseri
7. equus pulcher
8. equi pulchri
9. bellum miserum
10. bella misera

## Exercise 32.2

1. pecunia vestra
2. pecunia nostra
3. libri vestri
4. libri nostri
5. scuta vestra
6. scuta nostra
7. dominus vester
8. domini nostri
9. servi vestri
10. sagittae nostrae

## Exercise 32.3

1. ancillam miseram habeo.
2. hortum pulchrum specto.
3. equos vestros video.
4. dominum nostrum amo.
5. vina pulchra bibo.

## Exercise 32.4

1. villam pulchram habebam.
2. librum bonum legebat.
3. templa pulchra spectabamus.
4. ancillas miseras non laudabam.
5. forum pulchrum delebant.

## Exercise 32.5

1. The queen often used to praise our allies.
2. The miserable slaves were running out of the beautiful temple.
3. Farmers, the allies are attacking your villas and destroying your fields!
4. Masters, why do you never praise your slaves?
5. We often used to drink good wines in our garden.

## Exercise 32.6

1. puella me amat.
2. dominus nos amat.
3. te amo.
4. nos amant.
5. vos non amant.
6. regina nos spectat.
7. dominus te audit.
8. poeta vos laudat.
9. domina nos iubet.
10. te rogo.

## Exercise 32.7

1. You are a good girl, I am a bad girl.
2. I was holding spears, you were holding arrows.
3. I like you, but you do not like me.
4. Allies, we love you!
5. You were running, we were walking.
6. I am miserable because girls do not like me.
7. You are bad maidservants, I am a good mistress.
8. Boys are always looking at me because I am a beautiful girl.
9. Why was the teacher never praising me?
10. The teacher was never praising you because you never used to work.

## Exercise 33.1

Romulus and Remus and their friends came to a river. The name of the river was the Tiber. The boys and their friends decided to build their new town in this place. Near the river were seven hills. Romulus climbed the first hill, Remus climbed the second hill. The boys were now tired. They stood here and waited for a sign of the gods.

## Exercise 33.2

1. a. et
   b. aedificare
   c. erat/erant
   d. iam/hic/non/diu/ubi/deinde
   e. (nomen)/oppidum/signum/caelo
2. Accusative. After the preposition ad.
3. Masculine.
4. Remus
5. aquilas

## Exercise 34.1

1. cucurri.
2. cepisti.
3. duxit.
4. rexistis.
5. dedit.
6. manserunt.
7. cucurrimus.
8. monuit.
9. misimus.
10. fuerunt.

## Exercise 34.2

1. dedimus.
2. duximus.
3. cucurrit.
4. monuisti.
5. fuit.
6. mansit.
7. cucurrerunt.
8. dedistis.
9. pugnaverunt.
10. rexit.

## Exercise 34.3

1. The horse ran well.
2. The slaves stayed for a long time.
3. The queen ruled well.
4. The boys were good.
5. The husband sent money.
6. The sailors liked the queen.
7. The master warned the slaves.
8. The Greeks captured the Troy.
9. The maidservant loved the dangers.
10. The inhabitants ruled the land.

## Exercise 34.4

1. equi ibi manserunt.
2. servi bene pugnaverunt.
3. regina numquam bene rexit.
4. scuta magna erant/fuerunt.
5. nauta cibum misit.
6. servus dominum amavit.
7. dominus epistulam amavit.
8. servi equos duxerunt.
9. amici verba audiverunt.
10. regina insulam cepit.

## Exercise 34.5

1. The girls stayed in the garden for a long time.
2. The master gave money to the slaves.
3. The woman warned the boys about the dangers.
4. The horses of the master ran into the fields.
5. The slaves sent wine to their master.
6. The sailor led the horse out of the field.
7. Many maidservants gave money to the good master.
8. The slave of the master was angry and wicked.
9. The allies captured many prisoners in the savage battle.
10. The small boy ran out of the big temple of the gods.

## Exercise 35.1

Romulus said these words to Remus: 'Remus, did you see the eagles? I saw twelve eagles. You only saw six. I shall therefore build our new town in this place. This place is sacred.' When Remus heard Romulus' words he was angry. He replied to Romulus: 'Are you mad, Romulus? I saw my six eagles before you saw your twelve eagles. I therefore, not you, shall build the new town.' The boys were not happy. And so Romulus and Remus and their allies argued among themselves.

## Exercise 35.2

1. a. verba/oppidum
   b. duodecim/sex
   c. nostrum/novum/sacer/iratus/insanus/meas/tuas/laeti
2. Dative.
3. Perfect.
4. Subject: Remus. Object: verba.
5. sum
6. 1st person. Singular.

## Exercise 36.1

1. Are they laughing?
2. Is he singing?
3. Are we attacking?
4. Are you playing?
5. Was he writing?
6. Were they sleeping?
7. Were we sailing?
8. Did you see?
9. Did they fight?
10. Did he stay?

## Exercise 36.2

1. puellaene rident?
2. dominusne dormit?
3. servine laborabant?
4. amicusne veniebat?
5. virine discesserunt?
6. filiusne audiebat?
7. puerne risit?
8. libertine timebant?
9. agricolaene oppugnaverunt?
10. filiane bibit?

## Exercise 36.3

1. Does the boy like the girl?
2. Did the teacher eat the food?
3. Were the slaves drinking wine?
4. Did the inhabitants build the temple?
5. Were the men carrying shields?

## Exercise 36.4

1. puellaene pueros semper amant?
2. agricolane equos in agrum duxit?
3. ancillaene in horto ludebant?
4. agricolaene in agro diu manserunt?
5. dominusne pecuniam servis ostendebat?

## Exercise 37.1

Romulus and Remus were arguing. Remus and his allies decided to build their new town on the Aventine Hill. Romulud and his allies decided to build their walls on the Palatine Hill. One day Remus visited Romulus' town. Romulus showed the walls of his town to Remus. When Remus saw Romulus' walls, he laughed. He even ran to Romulus and shouted: 'Your walls are small, not strong. They will never protect your town well! Who built these?' When the cruel Romulus heard Remus' words he was very angry. Suddenly he took his sword, he ran towards Remus, (and) he killed him with his sword.

## Exercise 37.2

1. a. suum/novum/suos/sui/tui/parvi/validi/tuum/saevus/iratus
   b. sunt/erat
   c. olim/numquam/bene/magnopere/subito
2. Infinitive.
3. Subject: Remus. Object: oppidum.
4. Accusative. Object of the verb.
5. capio.
6. Ablative.

## Exercise 38.1

1. Where are the boys? They are away.
2. When the teacher is away, the boys and girls like to play.
3. The slaves were not working because the master was away.
4. Many men were present in the town.
5. Why were you away, boy? I was away because I did not want to work.
6. The woman's husband was away for a long time.
7. The slave always works well when his master is present.
8. Why were you not present in the villa, maidservants?
9. We were not present in the villa because we were working in the fields.
10. Many farmers are always present in the fields.

## Exercise 38.2

1. multi amici in villa aderant.
2. pueri, quod magister aberat, non laborabant.
3. amice, cur in foro non aderas?
4. in foro non aderam quod in oppido non eram.
5. puellae saepe afuerunt.

## Test 1

1. reginam amamus.
2. hastae necant.
3. servos non saepe necamus.
4. villam non habeo.
5. reginam timeo.

## Test 2

1. villam et pecuniam habet.
2. puella regina non est.
3. viam aedificamus.
4. ancilla cenam parat.
5. nautae semper clamant.

## Test 3

1. epistulam vides.
2. dominus servos non timet.
3. villam delemus.
4. feminae muros non aedificant.
5. servi pecuniam non saepe habent.

## Test 4

1. servi viam aedificant.
2. reginae deos timent.
3. dominus servum necat.
4. feminam et filium amo.
5. regina deos timet.

## Test 5

1. nautae libros amant.
2. pueri semper clamant.
3. libros amamus.
4. gladios habemus.
5. pueri hastas non saepe portant.

## Test 6

1. servi cenam parant.
2. domini villas et servos habent.
3. servi viam aedificant.
4. pueri sunt.
5. vir murum aedificat.

## Test 7

1. servus librum amat.
2. puellae magistrum timent.
3. dei templa amant.
4. vir puellam videt.
5. regina templum intrat.

## Test 8

1. oppida et villas amamus.
2. filius vinum amat.
3. deos amamus.
4. pueri libros non saepe amant.
5. regina non est.

Tests 9 – 18  Nova Latina 1 Specimen Answers

## Test 9

1. deos timemus.
2. magistri pueros non necant.
3. libros et epistulas amamus
4. Romani sunt.
5. equos saepe spectamus.

## Test 10

1. ancilla cenam parabat.
2. magister libros semper portat.
3. puellae saepe clamabant.
4. dominus villam et equos habet.
5. magister pueros laudabat.

## Test 11

1. dominus ancillam monebat.
2. vir feminam spectabat.
3. ancillae dominum non amant.
4. amicum non habet.
5. Romani vias et oppida aedificabant.

## Test 12

1. servi templa aedificabant.
2. nauta gladium et hastam habet.
3. dominus cenam laudabat.
4. puella nautam timebat.
5. oppidum non intras.

## Test 13

1. servus pecuniam portabat.
2. amicus hastam et gladium habet.
3. templa spectabant.
4. equus virum portat.
5. pueri et puellae reginam spectabant.

## Test 14

1. magistri amicos non saepe habent.
2. dei Romanos monebant.
3. viri nautae erant.
4. puer librum laudabat.
5. regina epistulam habet.

## Test 15

1. magistri saepe monent.
2. pecuniam spectabamus.
3. Romani gladios portabant.
4. pueri magistrum amant.
5. servi murum aedificabant.

## Test 16

1. filius vinum et cenam amat.  !!!
2. Romani murum delebant.
3. dominus equos vocabat.
4. servus magistrum timebat.
5. nauta pecuniam portabat.

## Test 17

1. Romani vina amabant.
2. templa saepe spectamus.
3. servi dominum timebant.
4. ancillae non sumus.
5. viri et feminae clamabant.

## Test 18

1. vir deos laudabat.
2. oppidum aedificabamus.
3. magister pueros et puellas laudabat.
4. Romani oppida delebant.
5. servi villas aedificant.

Printed in Great Britain
by Amazon